NATIONAL GEOGRAPHIC

Ladders

Speak Out

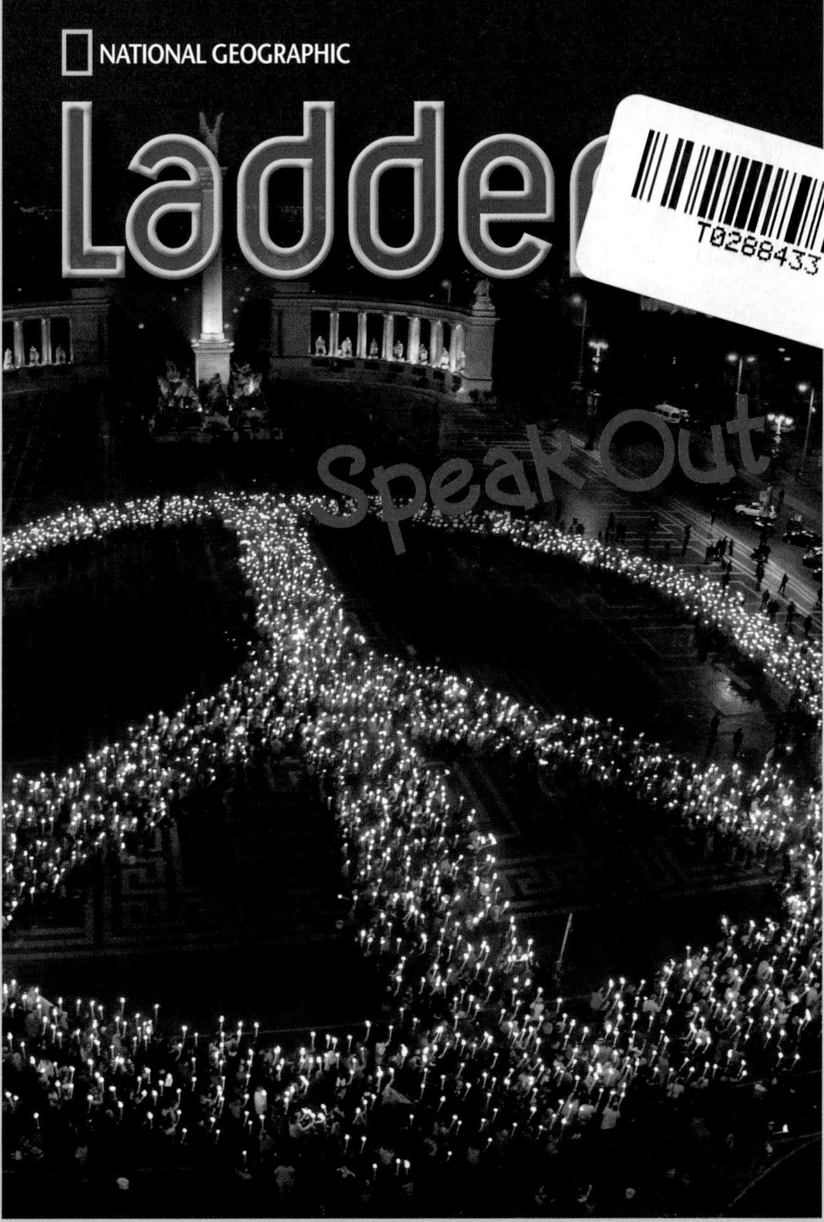

GENRE Social Studies Article

Read to find out about communication methods across time.

Getting the Word Out

by Barbara Keeler

Communication in Early Civilization

Nobody knows when humans first began to **communicate,** but they may have begun to express themselves almost 5,400 years ago. Their first messages might have taken the form of art on the walls of caves.

Primitive people used different ways to communicate over limited distances. Smoke signals sent messages as far as the eye could see, and drums sent messages as far as the ear could hear.

People were probably speaking long before they were writing. Without writing, it was hard to preserve messages over time and send them beyond the range of sight and hearing. An oral message sent a distance, or passed to succeeding generations, was only as accurate as the memory of specific humans.

After early people invented writing, ideas and information could be preserved, copied, and sent to people in other places. Communication could be **transmitted** accurately over time and between locations.

This type of ancient writing is called *Cuneiform*. It was used in Mesopotamia.

These cave paintings in Lascaux, France are about 17,000 years old.

15,000 B.C.

around 15,000 B.C. earliest known cave paintings at Lascaux, France

5000 B.C.

between 3400 and 3200 B.C. earliest known Egyptian writing

about 3200 B.C. earliest writing in Mesopotamia

ord out

At first, written messages were carved into or written on hard surfaces or animal skins. Then the Egyptians invented paper-like sheets made from the papyrus plant. With lighter weight writing material, written messages could be easily carried over a distance.

Egyptians began to use a postal service around 2000 B.C. About 600 B.C., Persians sent messages using a system of mounted messengers. Horseback riders worked in relay, stopping at regularly placed stations to change horses or pass their messages to another rider.

Pigeons could also carry messages on lightweight material. Mesopotamians used carrier pigeons as early as 2500 B.C.

Egyptians made the paper-like papyrus from leaves of the papyrus plant.

This ancient Mayan text was written between 300 and 200 B.C.

about 3000 B.C.
Egyptians use papyrus sheets for writing

about 2000 B.C.
postal service in Egypt

2500 B.C.

0

2500 B.C.
carrier pigeons carry messages in Mesopotamia

400–300 B.C.
earliest known writing in Central America

105 B.C.
paper invented in China

Printing Spreads the Word

After years of rolling papyrus into scrolls, people began binding pages of paper into books. Books were easier to store and move around than scrolls.

The problem with books was that each page had to be written by hand. If someone wanted a copy of a book, it could take years to copy it by hand. Therefore, few books were available, so most people had no reason to learn to read.

In 1455, Johannes Gutenberg invented a printing press. Unlike earlier printing blocks of whole words, this press had movable inked letters. Now printers could form an unlimited amount of words. In less time than it had taken to hand copy one book, printers could publish thousands of copies.

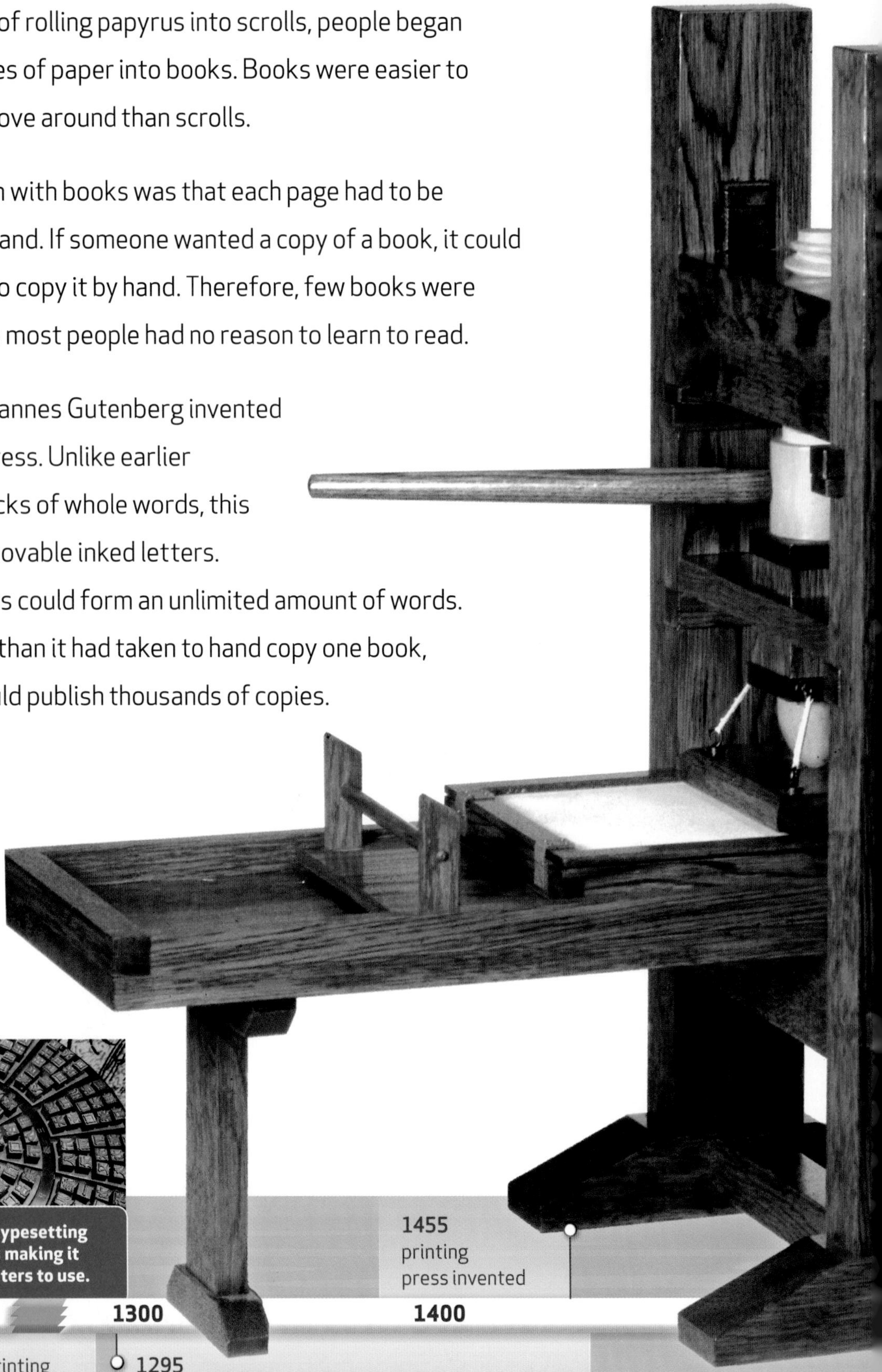

This Chinese typesetting plate revolves making it easier for printers to use.

100

Chinese printing blocks invented

1300

1295
Marco Polo returned to Italy from China and brought along the understanding of block-letter printing. Italians began to use block letters for printing.

1400

1455
printing press invented

As a result more people had access to information and ideas. Books became the primary tool for learning, so more people learned to read.

Printing current news and events also became possible with the printing press. The first daily newspaper was published in 1650. Later when the typewriter was invented, ordinary people could type messages much faster than they could write by hand. According to many historians, American author Mark Twain was the first author to submit a typewritten book manuscript in 1883.

Gutenberg adapted an olive oil press to create his printing press. He used metal blocks. They were long lasting and easy to move.

1650
first daily newspaper published in Leipzig, Germany

1874
first typewriters placed on the market

1700 **1800** **1900**

This typewriter was produced around 1878. It was the first model that could print both lower and upper case letters.

Early Telecommunications

Even after writing and printing were invented, spreading messages was still slow and difficult. Messages could only be sent by existing forms of transportation. Oral or written, messages could not travel faster than the fastest person, animal, or boat.

For example, the Declaration of Independence was printed in early July of 1776, but did not reach England until August 10, 1776.

During the 1830s, inventors found a way to transmit messages over wires using signals called *Morse Code*. A person on the receiving end translated the signals into words on a paper document called a telegram. The telegraph, as the invention was called, sent messages instantly from one end of the country to another. Wires soon connected all major United States' cities, and cables were laid under the Atlantic Ocean. Sometimes newspapers could publish news from across the world on the day events took place.

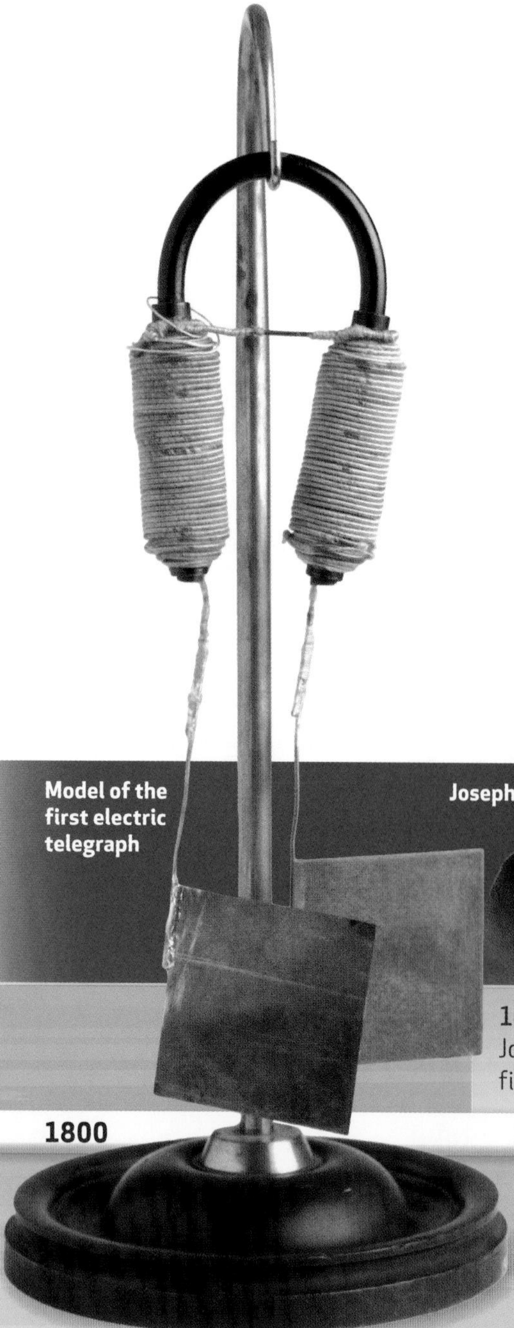

Model of the first electric telegraph

Joseph Henry

Morse code uses short and long pulses to represent letters and numbers. Sounds, lights, or written dots and dashes are all used for communicating Morse code. A "dot" is a short pulse. A "dash" is a long pulse.

● ● ● ▬ ▬ ▬ ● ● ●

S O S

1800

1832
Joseph Henry invents the first electric telegraph.

1820

1835
Samuel Morse and Alfred Vail invent Morse code.

1840

1844
The first long-distance electric telegraph line is constructed between Baltimore, MD and Washington, DC.

Later that century, another invention made it possible to speak directly to someone miles away. In 1876, crowds gathered at a telegraph office and took turns singing and reciting into a telephone receiver. In another telegraph station six miles away, the inventor of the telephone, Alexander Graham Bell, listened to their words.

By 1880 about 30,000 telephones were in use in the United States. By 1915 telephone lines stretched from coast to coast.

Tele-Everything

The names for the new communication devices weren't just clever word play. The inventors used Greek and Latin word parts to name their new devices.

Tele- means *distant* or *over a distance;* *-gram* means *writing* or *recording;* *phone* comes from *phon* or *phono* and means *sound, voice,* or *speech.*

The first phones used a single hole for speaking and listening. To call another phone, a person stuck a finger into the hole and scratched a metal plate. If the other person heard the scratching on the other phone, he or she would respond.

1860 **1880** **1900**

1876
first telephone call

1892
Alexander Graham Bell makes first cross-country call from New York to Chicago.

Up to the Minute Communications

The telegraph and telephone could only send messages between places that were connected by wires. These devices were of no use to a ship at sea or to someone in a desert or forest. During the 1900s, however, scientists learned to send messages without wires through the air. In 1901, wireless telegraph messages were sent across the Atlantic Ocean. In 1906, advancements made vocal transmission possible. Two people could talk to each other on wireless radios, even if they were on ships or in the desert. The advancement of sending wireless messages laid the foundation to develop portable wireless phones.

At first, radios were used for two-way conversations. After a commercial station began to send one-way radio **broadcasts** to larger audiences, people began to buy radios for their homes. Later cars came with radios installed. Radios became a major source of news. Events could be reported within a shorter period of time, even the same day or hour of the occurrence. People also relied on radio broadcasts for music and entertainment.

Later models of radios were small enough to be set on tabletops. Just like today, finding ways to reduce the size of pieces of technology was an example of technological progress.

Early radios were built like cabinets and stood in corners of homes like pieces of furniture.

1900 — 1910 — 1920

1906 first experimental radio broadcast

first commercial radio station launched

1921 first World Series baseball game broadcast via radio

With the invention of television, photographs and moving pictures could be broadcast as well as sound. People stared in wonder at the television set that was unveiled at the 1939 World's Fair. As amazing as television was, the use of radio was much more widespread.

A decade later, television's popularity and accessibility had grown. Along with television's popularity came the power to influence. The television commercials, news, and entertainment began to shape people's opinions, tastes, and attitudes.

1930 | 1940 | 1950

1939 first television demonstrated at the New York World's Fair

In the early 1940s, TVs became smaller and no longer took up space in homes like large pieces of furniture.

The Computer Age

The computer age revolutionized communication again. Military researchers developed computers during World War II. By the late 1960s, many government agencies were using computers. With computers, people could do their written work faster and store it in the computer. Even so, people could still not access and share written information as easily as they wanted. For written information, people turned to published books, newspapers, or magazines. If they did not own the resource, they had to go to a library, that is, until the Internet was available.

The first computers were enormous and costly.

1946
first general-purpose, all-electronic computer

1950

1960

1960
first video game created: *SpaceWar!*

1969
early form of the Internet created

1970

1971
electronic mail, or e-mail, invented

During the 1960s, researchers developed a system that allowed computers to share information over wires. In 1969, they created an early form of the Internet, and computers at universities and government agencies began exchanging data. By 1971, engineers created electronic mail, or e-mail. Later computers were able to share data without wires. A vision of laptop computers was also part of this era. The DynaBook was such an idea. The DynaBook was intended to be a children's learning tool, but it was never made. A decade later, in the early 1980s, the first laptops were produced and sold.

Later in the 1990s, a world-wide **network** of computers was developed to share information and this launched the *World Wide Web*. Web service providers began to connect millions of businesses and homes to each other.

The personal computer and the Internet transformed the world dramatically. People had access to more information than ever before. They used the Internet for research, shopping, and sending messages. They played games online and set up commercial and personal Web sites.

The Internet also enabled the use of "cloud computing." At first, cloud computing was used for e-mail and to store data online. Later it expanded to include using online software and applications.

With the Internet, people could reach ever-wider audiences. To publish in print media, a writer had to get past a "gatekeeper," someone who decided and chose the writing. Now personal Web sites allow ordinary people to bypass the traditional "gatekeepers" and instantly communicate to and with broad audiences.

1983
battery operated portable computer sold by major U.S. electronics store

1984
first cell phone sold for $3,995 with a half hour of talk time

1980

The first personal computers in the late 1970s had awkward keyboards and small screens.

1990

The design of desktop computers in the 90s included a keyboard and screen setup that was comfortable for most users even though keys were chunky and the monitor was heavy.

From Your Hand to the World

The burst of technological development in the 70s, 80s, and 90s, which included personal computers, email, and the Internet, ushered communication technology into the Millennium. Laptop computers became lighter and more powerful. The first tablet-style computer hit stores in 2002, but consumers didn't immediately jump to purchase them until after 2009.

At the start of the Millennium, cellular phones became the latest communication device. It's important to recall how different life was before cell phones were so widely used. People could not call friends or family who were outdoors, traveling, or away from a phone line. People who were lost or in an accident on a deserted roadway could not call for help. Family members on the go could not easily keep in touch with one another. To call home, they needed to find a pay phone and deposit coins to dial.

Today cell phones are so small and widely available that most Americans carry them, including some children. Many homes no longer feature landlines for telephone communication. Cell phones are capable of sending text messages and taking pictures or videos. Newer versions of cell phones, called smartphones, are small enough to be carried in a pocket, but offer the benefits of a phone, a camera, and a computer with Internet access. Applications allow people to shop, watch films, hear music, do research, and keep in touch with their friends, even through video.

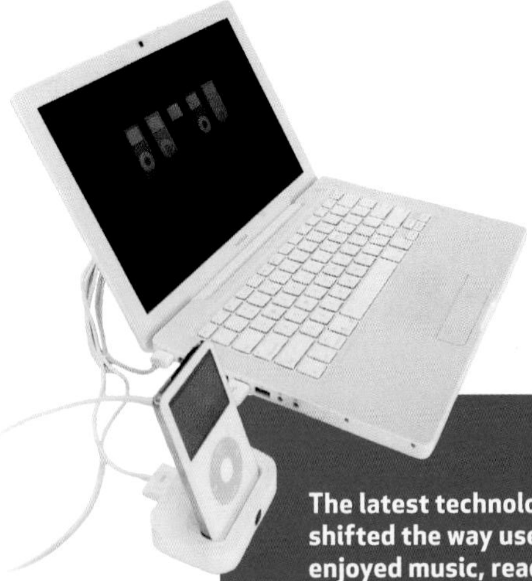

The latest technology shifted the way users enjoyed music, read for pleasure, and socialized.

Cell phones are often used to take and send photos.

2000

2002
first cell phones with cameras

2003
Libraries begin offering free downloadable e-books.

2004
first e-ink based e-book reading device

2005

First generation e-ink reader

New ways to share opinions, news, stories, and photos developed because of the Internet. An era of making your personal experiences public or semi-public was launched with the use of blogs and social media. People could and can still connect with friends and family any minute of the day, regardless of where each person lives.

From their earliest attempts at communication, people have revolutionized the process with their inventions. Writing systems and printing presses changed the world and people's lives. The telegraph, telephone, radio, and television delivered messages worldwide. The Internet and smartphones propelled people into an age where communication, information, and entertainment were instantaneous. No one really knows what the future holds. What's certain is that devices we use to communicate will continue to evolve, and new inventions will spring from devices we now carry in a backpack, put in a pocket, or hold in our hand.

With the onset of touch screens, tablet users can do with finger swipes what keyboards used to do.

Teens and adults communicate as much or more by short written texts. Users often decide to write rather than talk.

2010

2011
first smart phone used on spacecraft

Check In What surprised you about communication inventions from the past?

GENRE History Article   **Read to find out** about spoken messages that made history.

The Power of Speech

by John Manos

Unifying a Nation

Speeches have tremendous power. Well-chosen words delivered by a good speaker can move people in a way that is unmatched by almost anything else. Often it is not only the way the speaker delivers the words that makes a speech historic but also the events happening in the world at the time it is given.

Great oration, or speaking, is not a natural talent of every leader. But one job of presidents and other elected officials is to unify a nation in a time of crisis. These are moments when a whole nation of people needs to draw together. And it is in these moments that the power of a speech is at its greatest. Throughout history, many memorable speeches have been given in times of national **crisis.**

A time in history known as *The Great Depression* had cost a quarter of the American people their jobs. It looked as though prosperity would never return to the country. It was into this climate that Franklin Delano Roosevelt was elected president in 1932. FDR, as he was known, delivered his first **inaugural** address on March 4, 1933, which was broadcast across the country. Ever since, people have quoted a single phrase from the speech:

"the only thing we have to fear **is fear itself.**"

During the Depression, people stood in long lines for food. One out of every four people was without a job.

During his presidency, FDR combined the power of speech with one of the most important **communication** tools of the day: the radio. American homes would not have televisions widely in use until a more than a decade later. But radio use was spreading. FDR's radio speeches were known as the "Fireside Chats." Americans at the time felt that they knew the President almost as a personal friend. FDR spoke in a manner that brought security and comfort but also roused and encouraged. FDR asked listeners to communicate to him in response to his speeches. And people did. Millions of letters were sent and received. Roosevelt used the power of his voice and also crafted language that everyone could understand. He used anecdotes and analogies. He helped lift up the spirits of citizens during a devastating time. And because of the special care in crafting and delivering the radio broadcasts, FDR was persuasive and well respected by citizens. He used language that created a national identity, where everyone was a part of the same team, one that hoped in his words: *"Together we cannot fail."*

Roosevelt made 31 live radio speeches during his presidency.

Speeches can also unify people in times of celebration. Such speeches often call attention to a shared sense of purpose. Many speeches that are given to **commemorate** an important event become a kind of rallying cry for an entire population. When John Fitzgerald Kennedy was elected president in 1962 at age 43, he was the youngest person ever elected to the office. He brought an image of youthful energy to his inaugural address, and he stated it directly, saying:

"Let the word go forth from this time and place, to friend and foe alike, that the torch has been passed to a new generation of Americans."

In his speech, Kennedy described challenges he felt the country faced, and he called upon all to offer their own efforts to meet those challenges. At the end of the speech, he delivered a line that is still often quoted:

"And so, my fellow Americans, ask not what your country can do for you, ask what you can do for your country."

President Barack Obama

Speeches that unify a nation may bring us together to commemorate historic firsts. On January 20, 2009, Barack H. Obama became the first African American to be elected President of the United States. He spoke to some 1.8 million people in Washington, D.C. that day. He recalled the journey of earlier Americans. His words asked Americans to continue on in the same spirit:

". . . it has been the risk-takers, the doers, the makers of things . . . who have carried us up the long, rugged path towards prosperity and freedom. . . . This is the journey we continue today."

Human and Civil Rights

Some speeches mark a moment in history, as they did during The Great Depression, or when a new president takes office. At other times, a great speech can change history. This has been especially true in the long worldwide struggle to achieve human and civil rights.

There is no better example of a civil rights speech than the "I Have a Dream" speech delivered by Martin Luther King, Jr. on August 28, 1963. It is considered one of the greatest speeches in U.S. history. A century after African Americans had been freed from slavery, they still were denied basic freedoms in many parts of the country. Dr. King offered a vision of hope and change in an electrifying speech that helped reshape the course of our entire American society:

"I have a dream that one day this nation will rise up and live out the true meaning of its creed: 'We hold these truths to be self-evident, that all men are created equal.'

I have a dream that one day on the red hills of Georgia, the sons of former slaves and the sons of former slave owners will be able to sit down together at the table of brotherhood."

"I have a dream that my four little children will one day live in a nation where they will not be judged by the color of their skin but by the content of their character."

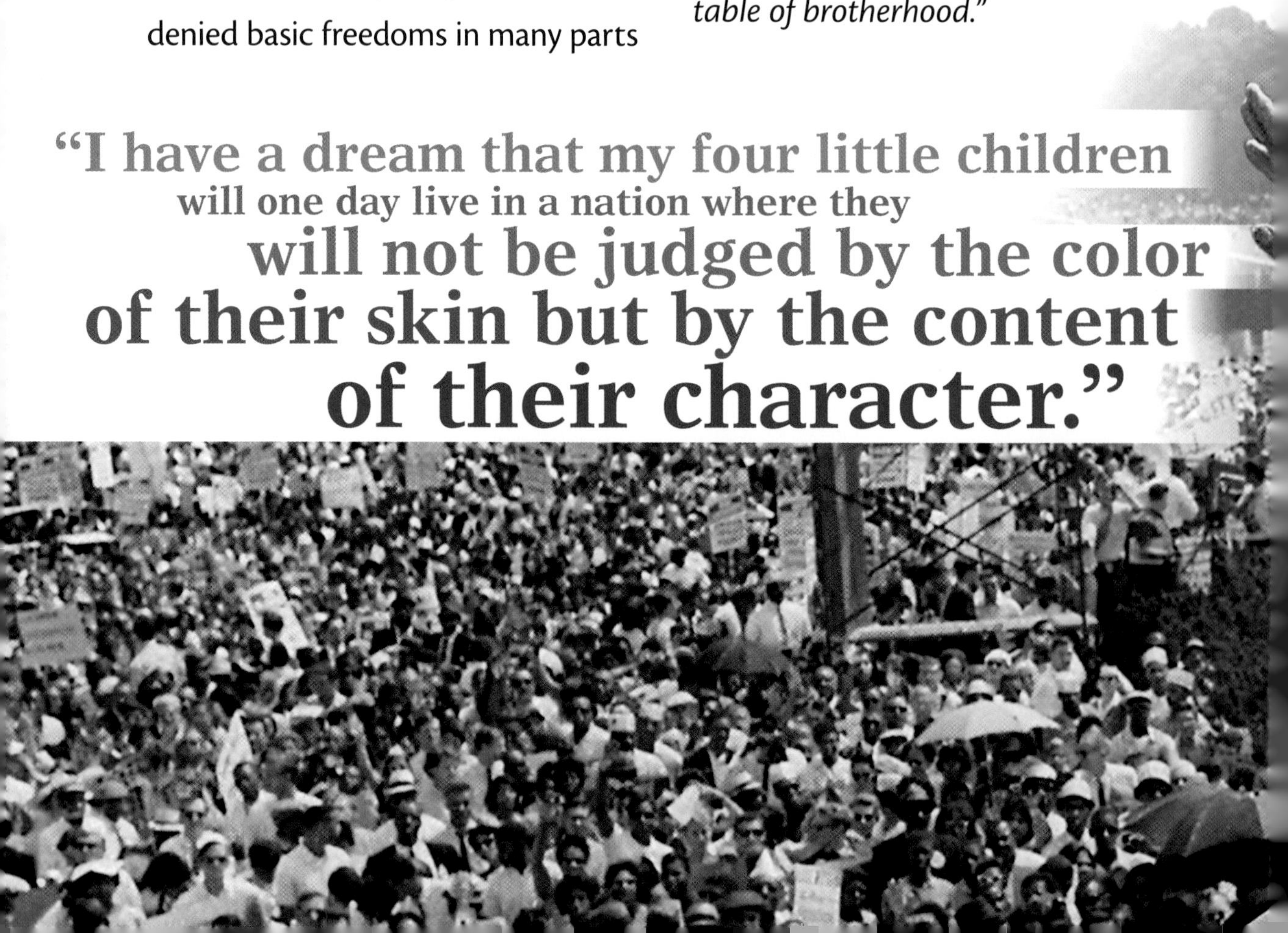

Mohandas Gandhi of India was one of Dr. King's heroes. Gandhi believed that the only way to achieve lasting civil rights was through nonviolent means. On August 8, 1942, in Bombay (now Mumbai) he described his goals:

"Ours is not a drive for power but purely a nonviolent fight for India's independence . . . In the democracy which I have envisaged, a democracy established by nonviolence, there will be equal freedom for all. Everybody will be his own master."

Mohandas Gandhi

Sandra Day O'Connor

Great Feats and Broken Barriers

Great accomplishments, important events, and falling barriers all lead to great speeches. We honor such achievements through speeches as they occur and afterward in remembrances.

In 1981, President Ronald Reagan nominated Sandra Day O'Connor as the first female Supreme Court Justice in U.S. history. In a speech she gave 23 years later in 2004, O'Connor described herself as "a cowgirl from eastern Arizona" noting that life had led her to amazing experiences. She commemorated the nomination saying, *"...it was about women everywhere. It was about a nation that was on its way to bridging a chasm between genders that had divided us for too long."*

Some barriers are physical in addition to being political. One such case was the Berlin Wall, which was built overnight on April 13, 1961, during a time known as *The Cold War.* On June 12, 1987, President Ronald Reagan delivered a stirring speech in front of the main gate of the Berlin Wall. He spoke to the people trapped behind the Wall who could only hear his speech via illegal radio broadcasts. Reagan called on the leader of the Soviet Union, Mikhail Gorbachev, to make a profound change declaring, *"General Secretary Gorbachev, if you seek peace, if you seek prosperity for the Soviet Union and Eastern Europe, if you seek liberalization: Come here to this gate!"*

Reagan's speech is considered the beginning of the end of communism in Europe. Two years later, the Wall came down.

"Mr. Gorbachev, open this gate! Mr. Gorbachev, tear down this wall!"

Women's Voices

Throughout history, great speeches inspired many to take comfort, celebrate, or act in a new way. Important leaders, many of whom were men, gave such speeches, but so did women, and not only those who held political positions but also women who were common citizens. These women made history communicating in their own humble style.

Sojourner Truth

Sojourner Truth was such a woman. She was born into slavery, and when she was finally free, she spoke often about the rights of all people, particularly women. In 1851, she gave an extemporaneous, or unplanned, speech at a convention for women's rights. One issue of the day was whether women should be able to vote in a political election.

After a life of hard work in fields, Sojourner Truth knew she had abilities equal to men. *"Look at me! Look at my arm!"* she said. *"I have ploughed and planted, and gathered into barns, and no man could head me!"* This meant that no man could outdo her. At the time, if women were allowed to vote, there was the concern that only white women would be able to do so. Sojourner Truth wanted to communicate that all women, white and black, should have the right to the vote. She added thoughtfully, *"And ain't I a woman?"*

President Obama nominated Hillary Rodham Clinton to the role of U.S. Secretary of State in 2009. Before she played this role, Clinton had been a First Lady and a member of the U.S. Senate. One of the Secretary of State's responsibilities is to travel and speak to groups of international leaders and diplomats. In so doing, the Secretary of State delivers the United States' messages and policies around the world to international audiences. In the first three years as Secretary of State, Clinton traveled to over 90 countries, speaking often about the health and welfare of women and girls. In 2011, at a meeting focused on women, peace, and security, or safety, Clinton said, *"Many of us have tried to show the world that women are not just victims of war; they are agents of peace."* In this speech and others, Clinton used her role as a diplomat to educate and inform. She has stated that women are critical to making lasting changes that improve life for all people.

Hillary Rodham Clinton

"...when women organize in large numbers, they galvanize opinion and help change the course of history."

Words Today & Tomorrow

The spoken word has the power to move us. Speeches can persuade, entertain, inform, and inspire us. As was true throughout the past, great moments of the future will be made memorable through the words of future leaders, writers, entertainers, and ordinary people who are devoted to making life better for others.

"Women must try to do things as men have tried. When they fail, their failure must be but a challenge to others."

—**Amelia Earhart,** aviator

". . . you can have a dream, you can have struggles, but you can overcome those struggles through perseverance and the right mentors in your lives and (by) making good decisions."

—**John Herrington,** astronaut

“Your work is going to fill a large part of your life, and the only way to be truly satisfied is to do what you believe is great work. And the only way to do great work is to love what you do.”

—**Steve Jobs,** technology developer

“If you get, give. If you learn, teach.”

—**Maya Angelou,** poet

“Life is not a spectator sport. . . . If you’re going to spend your whole life in the grandstand just watching what goes on, in my opinion you’re wasting your life.”

—**Jackie Robinson,** baseball player and civil rights activist

Check In For what reasons have speeches been made throughout history?

GENRE How-To Article

Read to find out how to plan a presentation.

How to Plan a Presentation

by James Weber

So you need to prepare a presentation for your classmates, a club, or a group of family members? Here's a guide to doing just that and doing it well! Nearly everyone gets nervous before speaking to an audience. Choosing a topic you love, preparing your presentation with great research and a few visuals, and practicing your delivery will ensure success. It could be that you're able to persuade, inform, entertain, and even demonstrate, if required, all in one winning presentation. Clear **communication** is part of all kinds of jobs and many careers require some degree of public speaking. Getting comfortable speaking in front of audiences now is a great way to prepare for your future.

The word hieroglyph comes from two Greek words that mean *sacred* and *translations*. The earliest hieroglyphic inscription may have been written around 3400 B.C. In the 4th century A.D., a Roman emperor closed all Egyptian temples where many inscriptions could be read. The meanings of hieroglyphics were not deciphered again until the early 19th century.

You can ask your audience to try and write a message in hieroglyphics.

1 Choose Your Topic

If your presentation is for an assignment, you may have specific criteria to follow. However, building a presentation around a topic that fascinates you or a topic you know a lot about and enjoy, is the best way to go. Here's an example: *Coded messages throughout history.* Your presentation could use the broader topic of codes to present information about ancient communication that used a code, such as hieroglyphics. You might include information about Morse code, nautical flags, and other current communication codes. You could narrow your topic to make your presentation more specific. A well-focused topic helps you with your research and presentation notes.

U. S. Marine Navajo Code Talkers devised an unbreakable code. They developed a code of 411 military terms. The code included a full alphabet. For example, the Navajo word for *ice* is *tkin* and in the code it stood for the letter *I*. In 2001, all living Navajo Code Talkers received Congressional Medals of Honor for their work.

2 Plan and Research

You'll need to build your presentation with solid research. Great research will help you **articulate** the most interesting and important information. Focus your research goals on your topic and purpose, and search for interesting details that will entertain and educate your audience.

For example, your listeners may not know that during World War II, American Navajo Indians were expert "code talkers." You can explain what code talking was and how it was useful. Or you could demonstrate a series of Morse code exchanges. You might even be able to persuade your audience to conclude that today's use of text messages is a form of code talking.

Even though you'll be speaking during your presentation, you need to do some writing to prepare. The main goal of your writing is to find the best order, or flow, for your presentation. So if your presentation is a historical one, a good choice is to order your information chronologically. You might begin with ancient codes and work your way to present day. However, think about how to engage your audience. What will get your audience

You can create a code with a code dial. Substitute one letter of the alphabet for another. Spell out the new word. See if audience members can crack the code.

members' attention? You may want to start with an example such as an interesting code from any point in history. Or play a sound bite of Morse code beeps or a recording of Navajo code talkers. Then you'll need to find a way to transition back into the chronological flow.

Write speaking notes and revise and edit, just like you would for any piece of writing. Use your research to build the information you will present. Type up pieces of information, make slides, or even use note cards that you can easily hold during the presentation. Go over your final notes. Cut out details that aren't the most important or interesting, and find a catchy way to end the presentation.

Think about your materials and visuals. Will your audience want to participate? If so, have pens and paper available so they can try to write or break a code. Would a clear visual help you launch into your presentation? Design something that is easy to use. Watch out for cumbersome visuals that are hard to display. Have copies of any handouts prepared ahead of time, and test out all links to Web sites.

These flags are used as an international naval alphabet. Like other coded alphabets, each flag stands for a term. Sometimes the same flag stands for a letter. For instance, the blue and yellow striped flag stands for *Golf*. This term means "I require a pilot." It also stands for the letter *G*.

3 Practice

Gather all of your materials, including your written notes. Now use your voice. Practice reading through all of your notes, and speak loudly and clearly, just as you will during the actual presentation. Practice any difficult pronunciations. As you practice, demonstrate emotion and interest by using non-verbal communication. Gestures, facial expressions, and other mannerisms can convey information and enthusiasm.

Remember the purpose of your speech and set your tone to match. For example, if you want to inform and demonstrate, you can be serious and informational. If you are comfortable adding humor, have a lighthearted tone. No matter what, be yourself and your audience will respond positively. Being sincere and showing interest in the topic are powerful tools of persuasion.

Enlist a friend or family member to observe you as you rehearse and to point out distracting gestures such as lip biting or fidgeting. You can also practice before a mirror or, if possible, record and review yourself.

Now you are ready to launch your career as a presenter! Whatever your topic, you can plan and deliver a winning presentation when you follow these three steps to good public speaking.

Bring supplies for your listeners to make a nautical flag. Share the meanings of the colors and stripes. See if the group can read their meanings.

Helpful Tips

Relax. Take a deep breath to calm your nerves.

Smile. Before you begin your speech, smile and acknowledge your audience. This will **transmit** a warm, welcoming mood.

Project Your Voice. Speak slowly and clearly. Start off with a greeting, "good morning," "good afternoon," or even "hello."

Make Eye Contact. Calmly look around the whole room. As you speak, look directly at individual listeners for a few seconds.

Be confident. If you behave as if you are speaking from a position of authority, you will remain in control and be an effective presenter.

Check In Why is it important to plan a presentation?

Discuss Ideas

1. What connections can you make among the three pieces in *Speak Out*? How are the pieces related?

2. "Getting the Word Out" and "The Power of Speech" both present historical information. How did the writers of each selection organize the texts? What is alike and different about each text?

3. Use information from "Getting the Word Out" to share ways that communication devices changed over time. What changes do you think will happen in the future?

4. Look at the colorful quotations placed throughout "The Power of Speech." Choose one or two you like the most. What is it about the quote that appealed to you?

5. In "How To Plan a Presentation" the writer suggests activities related to codes that the audience could try. Which would you like to try and why?

6. What questions do you have about communication devices throughout history? What do you still want to learn more about?